IT'S TIME TO LEARN ABOUT OUR LADY OF GUADALUPE

It's Time to Learn about Our Lady of Guadalupe

Walter the Educator

Silent King Books
A WhichHead Entertainment Imprint

Copyright © 2024 by Walter the Educator

All rights reserved. No part of this book may be reproduced in any manner whatsoever without written permission except in the case of brief quotations embodied in critical articles and reviews.

First Printing, 2024

Disclaimer

The author and publisher offer this information without warranties expressed or implied. No matter the grounds, neither the author nor the publisher will be accountable for any losses, injuries, or other damages caused by the reader's use of this book. Your use of this book acknowledges an understanding and acceptance of this disclaimer.

It's Time to Learn about Our Lady of Guadalupe is a collectible little learning book by Walter the Educator that belongs to the Little Learning Books Series. Collect them all and more books at WaltertheEducator.com

OUR LADY OF GUADALUPE

INTRO

Our Lady of Guadalupe, or *La Virgen de Guadalupe*, holds a special place in the hearts and lives of millions, particularly within Mexican and Latino communities. She is more than a religious figure; she represents hope, identity, and cultural pride. Revered as the patroness of the Americas, Our Lady of Guadalupe's story is deeply intertwined with the history and traditions of Mexico, symbolizing a blend of indigenous heritage and Catholic faith. This little book delves into the history, symbolism, cultural significance, and continuing impact of Our Lady of Guadalupe, exploring how she has become a powerful emblem of faith, resilience, and unity for diverse communities around the world.

Historical Background

The story of Our Lady of Guadalupe begins in December 1531, a decade after the Spanish conquest of Mexico.

It's Time to Learn about Our Lady of Guadalupe

According to tradition, a native Mexican peasant named Juan Diego was walking near Tepeyac Hill, outside what is now Mexico City, when he encountered a radiant vision of the Virgin Mary.

It's Time to Learn about
Our Lady of Guadalupe

She appeared to him as a mestiza, a woman of mixed indigenous and European heritage, speaking to him in Nahuatl, the language of the Aztecs.

It's Time to Learn about Our Lady of Guadalupe

She identified herself as the Mother of the true God and asked that a church be built in her honor on the site.

It's Time to Learn about
Our Lady of Guadalupe

Juan Diego relayed the message to the local bishop, Juan de Zumárraga, who was skeptical and requested a sign. On December 12, after a series of miraculous events, Juan Diego returned to the bishop with his tilma, or cloak, which he had used to gather Castilian roses that the Virgin had miraculously provided, despite it being winter.

It's Time to Learn about
Our Lady of Guadalupe

When he opened his cloak, the roses fell to the ground, revealing an image of the Virgin imprinted on the fabric.

It's Time to Learn about
Our Lady of Guadalupe

This image, now enshrined in the Basilica of Our Lady of Guadalupe in Mexico City, has become one of the most venerated religious icons in the world.

It's Time to Learn about Our Lady of Guadalupe

Symbolism of the Image

The image of Our Lady of Guadalupe is rich with symbolism that resonates deeply with both Christian and indigenous traditions. Her appearance as a mestiza woman embodies a fusion of cultures and symbolizes the birth of a new people from the merging of indigenous and European bloodlines. The colors, patterns, and symbols in her depiction carry profound meanings:

It's Time to Learn about Our Lady of Guadalupe

1. **The Stars on Her Mantle**: The stars on her cloak are thought to correspond to the constellations visible in the sky on the date of her apparition, December 12, 1531. This celestial symbolism links her to both the heavens and the earth, reinforcing her role as a divine intercessor.

2. **The Sun and the Moon**: She is depicted standing atop a crescent moon, with rays of the sun surrounding her. In Aztec culture, the sun and the moon were powerful deities, and their depiction in this way suggests that she is more powerful than these gods, further emphasizing her divine nature.

3. **The Angel and the Colors**: An angel beneath her feet supports her, signifying her role as a messenger of God. The colors of her garments—turquoise and rose—are significant as well. Turquoise was a color of the Aztec nobility and divinity, while rose is associated with love and compassion.

4. **The Black Ribbon and Flowers**: The black ribbon around her waist indicates that she is with child, and the flower symbol over her womb, known as the Nahui Ollin, symbolizes the divine and central force of the universe. This suggests that she is carrying the Christ child, linking her to the Catholic tradition of the Virgin Mary as the mother of Jesus.

Cultural and Religious Significance

Our Lady of Guadalupe is not only a religious icon but also a cultural symbol that has played a pivotal role in shaping Mexican identity.

It's Time to Learn about Our Lady of Guadalupe

Her image and story have provided a unifying symbol for the people of Mexico and beyond, transcending the boundaries of religion and nationality.

It's Time to Learn about
Our Lady of Guadalupe

Indigenous and Spanish Influence

The appearance of the Virgin in the guise of an indigenous woman speaking Nahuatl was a powerful affirmation of the value and dignity of the indigenous people at a time when they were suffering under the harsh realities of Spanish colonial rule.

It's Time to Learn about Our Lady of Guadalupe

Her message of compassion and love was seen as a validation of the native population, who were often treated as inferior.

It's Time to Learn about
Our Lady of Guadalupe

This dual heritage has made her a powerful symbol of mestizaje, or the blending of indigenous and European cultures, which is central to Mexican identity.

It's Time to Learn about Our Lady of Guadalupe

Symbol of Independence and Social Justice

Throughout Mexican history, Our Lady of Guadalupe has been invoked as a symbol of justice and resistance.

It's Time to Learn about Our Lady of Guadalupe

During the Mexican War of Independence in the early 19th century, the revolutionary leader Miguel Hidalgo used the banner of the Virgin of Guadalupe as a rallying symbol for his troops.

It's Time to Learn about
Our Lady of Guadalupe

She was seen as a protector of the oppressed and a champion of liberation. In this context, she became not just a religious figure, but a symbol of national identity and social justice.

It's Time to Learn about
Our Lady of Guadalupe

Her image has continued to be a source of inspiration for social movements. For example, during the Chicano movement in the United States in the 1960s and 1970s,

It's Time to Learn about Our Lady of Guadalupe

Our Lady of Guadalupe was embraced as a symbol of pride and empowerment for Mexican Americans fighting for civil rights. Her image was used in protests and murals, representing the struggle for equality and the affirmation of cultural identity.

It's Time to Learn about Our Lady of Guadalupe

Patroness of the Americas

In 1945, Pope Pius XII declared Our Lady of Guadalupe as the "Queen of Mexico and Empress of the Americas."

It's Time to Learn about Our Lady of Guadalupe

Later, in 2002, Pope John Paul II canonized Juan Diego, affirming the validity and importance of the apparitions.

It's Time to Learn about
Our Lady of Guadalupe

The Virgin of Guadalupe is now venerated not only in Mexico but throughout the Americas, symbolizing the unity and shared faith of people across the continent.

It's Time to Learn about Our Lady of Guadalupe

Her basilica in Mexico City is one of the most visited Catholic pilgrimage sites in the world, drawing millions of devotees each year, particularly on her feast day, December 12. Pilgrims come to seek her intercession, offer thanks, and celebrate her enduring presence in their lives.

It's Time to Learn about
Our Lady of Guadalupe

The Scientific Enigma of the Tilma

The tilma of Juan Diego, with its miraculous image of Our Lady of Guadalupe, has been the subject of extensive scientific study and analysis.

It's Time to Learn about
Our Lady of Guadalupe

Despite being made of coarse cactus fibers, which should have deteriorated within a few decades, the tilma has remained intact for nearly 500 years. Researchers have been unable to explain the preservation of the fabric or the vividness of the colors, which appear to be neither paint nor dye.

It's Time to Learn about
Our Lady of Guadalupe

Examinations of the image have revealed other anomalies. For instance, the eyes of the Virgin in the image contain reflections that seem to depict scenes from the moment the tilma was presented to the bishop, a detail so minute it is difficult to see without magnification.

It's Time to Learn about
Our Lady of Guadalupe

This phenomenon has led some to believe that the image is not only miraculous in origin but also serves as a living testament to the veracity of Juan Diego's encounter.

It's Time to Learn about Our Lady of Guadalupe

Contemporary Devotion and Influence

Our Lady of Guadalupe continues to be a source of profound devotion and cultural influence. Her image is found not only in churches but also in homes, murals, tattoos, and even on clothing and jewelry. She is invoked in prayers for protection, healing, and guidance, and her feast day is celebrated with fervent devotion, featuring processions, Masses, and traditional dances.

It's Time to Learn about Our Lady of Guadalupe

A Unifying Force

In a world often divided by race, culture, and religion, Our Lady of Guadalupe stands as a unifying figure.

It's Time to Learn about Our Lady of Guadalupe

She bridges the gap between the indigenous and European, the rich and poor, the devout and the secular. Her message of love, compassion, and solidarity resonates across boundaries, offering hope and comfort to those who feel marginalized or oppressed.

It's Time to Learn about Our Lady of Guadalupe

Cultural Impact Beyond Religion

Our Lady of Guadalupe has also permeated popular culture. Artists, writers, and musicians have drawn inspiration from her story and image, using her as a symbol of beauty, resilience, and empowerment.

It's Time to Learn about Our Lady of Guadalupe

She has been portrayed in various forms of media, from literature to film, reflecting her multifaceted role as both a spiritual and cultural icon.

It's Time to Learn about Our Lady of Guadalupe

For many, especially in the Latino community, she represents a maternal figure who understands their struggles and offers solace. Her image is often present in times of personal or collective crisis, providing a sense of peace and assurance that they are not alone.

It's Time to Learn about
Our Lady of Guadalupe

OUTRO

Our Lady of Guadalupe is a symbol of faith, hope, and cultural identity that transcends time and borders. Her story, deeply rooted in both indigenous and Catholic traditions, reflects the complexities of Mexican history and the enduring spirit of its people. She is a testament to the power of faith to inspire and unite, offering a message of love and compassion that continues to resonate across the world.

In a society that is increasingly diverse and global, the enduring legacy of Our Lady of Guadalupe serves as a reminder of the importance of cultural and religious symbols in shaping our understanding of identity and belonging. She stands not only as a beacon of religious devotion but also as a powerful symbol of the unity and resilience of the human spirit. Her message, as relevant today as it was nearly 500 years ago, calls on us to embrace compassion, seek justice, and celebrate the richness of our shared humanity.

ABOUT THE CREATOR

Walter the Educator is one of the pseudonyms for Walter Anderson. Formally educated in Chemistry, Business, and Education, he is an educator, an author, a diverse entrepreneur, and he is the son of a disabled war veteran. "Walter the Educator" shares his time between educating and creating. He holds interests and owns several creative projects that entertain, enlighten, enhance, and educate, hoping to inspire and motivate you. Follow, find new works, and stay up to date with Walter the Educator™

at WaltertheEducator.com

www.ingramcontent.com/pod-product-compliance
Lightning Source LLC
LaVergne TN
LVHW051926060526
838201LV00062B/4699